W9-AHH-189

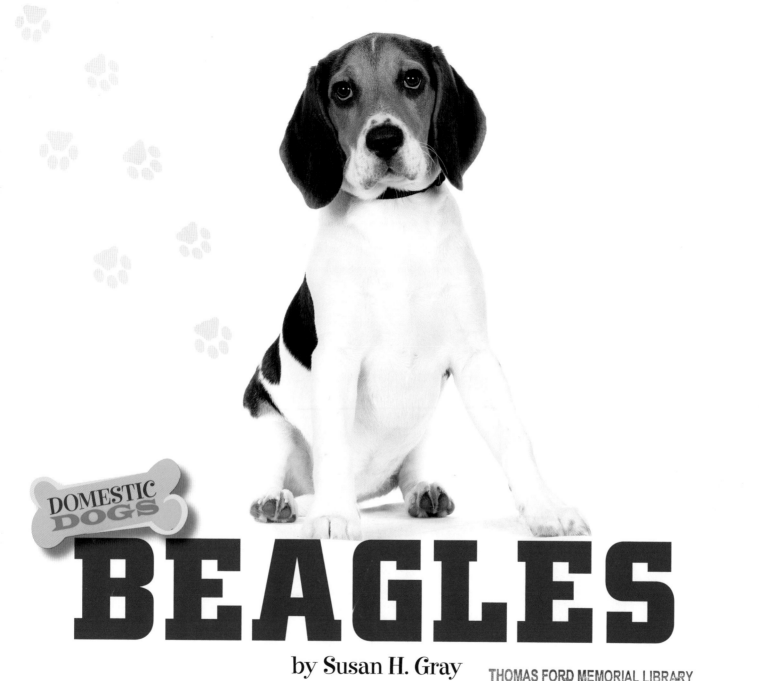

DOMESTIC DOGS

BEAGLES

by Susan H. Gray

Published in the United States of America by The Child's World®
1980 Lookout Drive • Mankato, Minnesota • 56003-1705
800-599-READ • www.childsworld.com

PHOTO CREDITS
© DLILLC/Corbis: 27
© Eric Isselée/BigStockPhoto.com: cover, 1
© Her Guy/BigStockPhoto.com: 15
© Historical Picture Archive/Corbis: 9
© iStockphoto.com/Willie B. Thomas: 29
© Jarvell Jardey/Alamy: 13
© Joe Raedle/Staff/Getty Images: 25
© Mark Raycroft/Minden Pictures: 11
© Purestock/Alamy: 17
© Rhonda O'Donnell/BigStockPhoto.com: 21
© Ron Hayes/Alamy: 23
© tbkmedia.de/Alamy: 19

ACKNOWLEDGMENTS
The Child's World®: Mary Berendes, Publishing Director;
Katherine Stevenson, Editor

The Design Lab: Kathleen Petelinsek, Design and Page Production

LIBRARY OF CONGRESS CATALOGING-IN-PUBLICATION DATA
Gray, Susan Heinrichs.
 Beagles / by Susan H. Gray.
  p. cm. — (Domestic dogs)
 Includes index.
 ISBN 978-1-59296-961-6 (library bound : alk. paper)
 1. Beagle (Dog breed)—Juvenile literature. I. Title. II. Series.
 SF429.B3G68 2008
 636.753'7—dc22   2007023030

Table of Contents

NAME That DOG!

What dog has a great sense of smell? What dog changes color as it gets older? What dog sometimes works at airports? What dog rolls around on stinky things? Did you guess the beagle? Then you are right!

5

An Uncertain History

No one is sure where beagles came from. About 1,800 years ago, beagle-like dogs lived in Great Britain (BRIH-tun). People from Rome had taken over the land. Perhaps they brought the dogs with them. No one knows for certain.

The dogs became **popular** in Britain. They had a good sense of smell. Hunters really liked them. The dogs were great for tracking hares. They tracked other small animals, too.

Great Britain is an island in Europe. It includes England, Scotland, and Wales. The map below shows where Great Britain is on Earth. The map on the right shows a closer view.

Atlantic Ocean

Scotland

North Sea

Northern Ireland

Ireland

England

Great Britain

Wales

Atlantic Ocean

English Channel

France

Even British kings and queens kept beagles. Queen Elizabeth the First had little pocket beagles. King Edward the Second had glove beagles. People said they were small enough to fit on a man's glove.

In the 1800s, a man named Phillip Honeywood lived in Britain. He took an interest in the dogs. He chose good hunters with a great sense of smell. Those dogs had puppies. Honeywood raised the puppies. He picked out the best hunters. He made sure *they* had puppies. This went on and on. In time, Honeywood had dogs who loved to track wild animals. They had an outstanding sense of smell. They liked to hunt in packs. They were a lot like the beagles we know today.

Soon, dog lovers brought beagles to America. These small dogs were excellent hunters. They quickly became popular in America. They are still popular today! In fact, they are America's fifth most popular **breed**.

This drawing is from 1820. It shows beagles tracking wild animals.

Little Hound Dogs

Beagles are small, sturdy, and handsome. Adults can be 15 inches (38 centimeters) tall at the shoulder. They weigh about 23 pounds (10 kilograms).

These dogs have short hair. The hairs feel hard to the touch. Most beagles have a three-color coat. The colors are black, white, and brown. Some beagles are just black and brown. Some are red and white. Others are tan and white. Often the tail has a white tip.

This beagle has a three-color coat.

Beagles look gentle and smart. Their soft, floppy ears hang down. Their eyes are brown or golden brown. They raise and lower their eyebrows. That can make them look sad or puzzled. It can make them look as if they are thinking hard.

Beagles belong to a group of dogs called *hounds*. Hounds are hunting dogs. They have an excellent sense of smell. They have lots of energy, too! They love to chase rabbits and squirrels.

Beagles and other hounds make baying sounds—"wah-oo," "woh," or "woo"! They make these sounds over and over. Hounds bay when they see other animals. They also bay when they are bored.

There are many kinds of hounds. Basset hounds and bloodhounds are well-known kinds. Dachshunds (DOX-hundts) and whippets are hounds, too.

This beagle is baying on a cloudy day.

13

Great Hunters, Great Pets

Beagles really love to hunt. They love to follow a **scent**. They like to chase squirrels and rabbits. They enjoy running with a pack of other beagles. Owners need to remember these things. They should walk their beagles on a leash. A beagle without a leash might run off! It might run after a squirrel. It might follow a scent all over the neighborhood. Those things can get the dog in trouble. It might get lost or hurt.

This beagle is following a scent in a city park.

How can you teach a beagle tricks? Give it some food when it does the right thing. Tell it, "Good dog!" That gives it a good reason to **obey** your commands.

Beagles like to be in a pack. If no other beagles are around, the family becomes their pack! Beagles love to be with their families. They want to run and play with the children. They do not want to be left alone.

Beagles like to think for themselves. Sometimes they are hard to train. They can be hard-headed and stubborn. They do not like to be bossed around. Owners must be **patient** when teaching them tricks. Beagles need a good reason to follow **commands**.

Beagles might be stubborn, but they make good pets. They love to be part of a family. They are easy to care for. They are friendly and **loyal**.

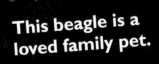

This beagle is a loved family pet.

Beagle Puppies

Beagle mothers often have six or seven puppies in a **litter**. Sometimes they have as many as 14! A newborn beagle weighs about one-half pound (one-fourth kilogram). That is about as heavy as a banana.

Newborn beagles do not bark or wag their tails. They do not play. They spend all their time sleeping or drinking their mother's milk.

These young beagles are drinking their mother's milk.

19

At first, the puppies' eyes are closed. The pups do not know if it is night or day. Their ears are not fully grown, either. They cannot hear their mother barking. They cannot hear their brothers and sisters whining.

The puppies grow quickly, though. After a month, they watch and hear everything. They run around and play together. That teaches them how to get along with other dogs.

Beagle puppies sometimes change color as they age. Black-and-white puppies might get brown patches as they get older. White puppies might turn into tan-and-white adults. Or they might turn red and white instead. People are often surprised to see their dogs change color!

Newborn beagles are small enough to fit into a person's hand.

This beagle puppy is a few weeks old.

These Dogs Really Smell!

Most owners love their beagles because they are such great pets. Hunters love them for their wonderful sense of smell. If an animal goes by, a beagle can smell it—even many hours later!

The insides of beagles' noses are especially good at smelling things. Beagles can smell lots of things that people cannot.

This beagle has found an interesting scent in the grass.

23

The United States government puts beagles' noses to work. The Beagle Brigade works in U.S. airports. A *brigade* is a group of workers. The workers in this brigade are all beagles! They are trained to sniff people's bags. They sniff out fruits, vegetables, and meats. Sometimes these foods carry germs or pests. Sneaking the foods into the U.S. is against the law. The beagles show their handlers which bags to search.

Beagles in the Beagle Brigade wear green vests. These dogs seem to like working in busy airports. They like to be around lots of people. And they love to sniff things!

This beagle works for the Beagle Brigade in Texas.

Caring for a Beagle

Beagles are strong, healthy little dogs. They are easy to care for. The main thing is to spend plenty of time with them. They love attention! They also love to go on long walks.

Beagles' long, floppy ears get dirty easily. Owners should check and clean the ears often. A beagle's coat needs some care, too. It should be brushed or combed once or twice a week. Baths are needed if the dog gets very dirty.

This beagle is getting a bath.

Beagles love to roll around in something smelly. Then they really need a bath!

Like all dogs, beagles can have health problems. Many beagles get heart problems as they grow older. Their hearts have trouble pumping blood through their bodies. Some beagles have a problem in their brain. The brain sends the wrong messages to the rest of the body. This causes the dog to have a **seizure**. The dog might fall over on its side. It might paddle its legs. **Veterinarians** can help beagles that have seizures.

Most beagles do not have such problems, though. They lead healthy, happy lives. They often live to be 12 or 13 years old. And they are fun to be around!

This veterinarian is making sure this beagle is healthy.

Glossary

breed (BREED) A breed is a certain type of an animal. Beagles are a well-known breed of dog.

commands (kuh-MANDZ) Commands are orders to do certain things. Food helps beagles learn commands.

litter (LIH-tur) A litter is a group of babies born to one animal. Beagle litters often have five to seven puppies.

loyal (LOY-ul) To be loyal is to be true to something and stand up for it. Beagles are loyal to their families.

obey (oh-BAY) To obey someone is to do what the person says. Beagles need a reason to obey.

patient (PAY-shunt) Being patient means facing problems without getting upset. Training beagles takes patience.

popular (PAH-pyuh-lur) When something is popular, it is liked by lots of people. Beagles are popular.

scent (SENT) A scent is a smell. Beagles love to follow a scent.

seizure (SEE-zhur) During a seizure, the brain sends wrong signals to the body. Some beagles have seizures.

veterinarians (vet-rih-NAIR-ee-unz) Veterinarians are doctors who take care of animals. Veterinarians are often called "vets" for short.

To Find Out More

Books to Read

American Kennel Club. *The Complete Dog Book for Kids.* New York: Howell Book House, 1996.

Kraeuter, Kristine. *Training Your Beagle.* Hauppauge, NY: Barron's Educational Series, 2001.

Mulvany, Martha. *The Story of the Beagle.* New York: PowerKids Press, 2000.

Roesel-Parent, Lucia. *Beagles.* Hauppauge, NY: Barron's Educational Series, 2003.

Sanford, William R., and Carl Green. *The Beagle.* New York: Crestwood House, 1990.

Vallila, Andew. *Beagle.* Philadelphia, PA: Chelsea House, 1999.

Places to Contact

American Kennel Club (AKC) Headquarters
260 Madison Ave, New York, NY 10016
Telephone: 212-696-8200

On the Web

Visit our Web site for lots of links about beagles:

http://www.childsworld.com/links

Note to Parents, Teachers, and Librarians: We routinely check our Web links to make sure they're safe, active sites—so encourage your readers to check them out!

Index

About the Author

Susan H. Gray has a Master's degree in zoology. She has written more than 70 science and reference books for children. She loves to garden and play the piano. Susan lives in Cabot, Arkansas, with her husband Michael and many pets.